ABC's

Neeli Cherkovski

SPUYTEN DUYVIL

New York City

The author wishes to thank Jason Morris for his editing on the text of Section One.

For more information on Neeli Cherkovski's writings, publications, and art, see www.neelicherkosvskipoet.com

© 2022 Neeli Cherkovski
ISBN 978-1-956005-34-9
Cover art by the author

Library of Congress Cataloging-in-Publication Data

Names: Cherkovski, Neeli, author.
Title: ABC's / Neeli Cherkovski.
Description: New York City : Spuyten Duyvil, [2022] |
Identifiers: LCCN 2021048647 | ISBN 9781956005349 (paperback)
Subjects: LCGFT: Poetry.
Classification: LCC PS3553.H3534 A63 2022 | DDC 811/.54--dc23
LC record available at https://lccn.loc.gov/2021048647

ABC's 1

for Ted Pearson

A

I sleep in a forest of funerals

my boat conquers the wild sea

tranquility retires for the duration
of our journey to Hell

pick a fight with the deep, fragrant woods

pine needles pulverize my dreams
as I rendezvous with noon, not a shade
in sight

night birds return

your mantle of riverbank grass torn
ass on magical reverberations
from the heat of common things,
don't you see how the diminutive chipmunk
may nibble for a lifetime on frigid seed?

my trees are filled with pages of an unfinished novel
so pleasing to the eye
it has horses and mountain trails
so many bumpy roads
animal tracks
amusing men with long white beards
amorous gardenias

acorn queen held her daughter's
hand under clamor of bees
out of every shire

moon songs, ethereal music and
stuff like that, the booksellers
were excited to see mercy back in print
quartz in a box reflecting numerous moods
letters wrapped in nature's kindness

keep moving in order to insure sweet shoes
and a light touch whilst thunder
crowds an atmosphere, pour letters

on empty lawn, not a churchyard
without stone signs, pleasing to hear
mummers in a procession
exposing the gratitude of the dead

ho! oh! ah! uh! poetry loves
the poverty-stricken sky, poets think
their roses don't smell, poets
dine on death, poets shiver in damp
closets like moths

under the lattice

A bowl, A table, A dog

Homeric bum
tossed out of Florence, another
shot by a firing squad, others gone
mad, some done-in by drink or
drug, oh poets you nightingales
in splendid storm, you've lived
to ransack the palaces
of men without honor

ANNEX TO A

aleph splendidly perched on leaf
from trees tended over three
and one-half decades

late Sunday morn—waiting
for birds to arrive—hoping
they'll show up to please
this plot of land—any bird
will do—may carry
yet another grain of aleph
proud Hebraic brick for
a tidal plain—trust various
levels of consciousness—
allow Nietzsche as messenger
for one level of mind—
who would be proper for
American earth? aleph beth
and gimel—sacred trinity
of sound spreading like
the song of songs—how simple
fervent bushes below—
one snail—green
slime on planks of the redwood deck

aleph yet hatchet in the skull
what a sample
what aging brain
wires up a motorcade? silent
branches—it took a moment
to stand aside as salt water
rueful and rustic poured over
the rocky coast—rip into

violence—ask for serenity—
a boy no more—restless back
mind lanterns to illumine
a shaft—ecstatic tree—unknown
bird—"pray for us sinners now"
in the Hebrew heaven—go find
the Musk Ox shaggy in a bank
of snow and ice—rest awhile
on the deck—why not amber
toward noon? what
lot of birds to come—
the deeper level—what does
the mind have in mind traces
of wood and feather—a faster grief
to hook, nerves to spare, anger
for a prize—ALEPH weighs-in,
jumping justice rags bricks of
the lower patio, oh how fine!

"A" at 17, sheltered by camellia
bushes brushing yellow stucco
walls, when was man created
in such a way he could speak?
how soon will the priesthood
drop in for a visit? we have
taken the liberty of stringing
letters on a thin strip of
paper, the typewriter wails,
the light is night when "A"
brays like a donkey, desolate
eyes scan the tree, the words
are woven from rich earth,
a spirit-sprite catches on in
time, at least, for the idea of

a bird—somehow they have
dinosaur brains—"I want to
love you," says the first bird
to appear, and to wade in
the soil and to move one more
letter to the sepulcher where
language lies, undaunted

B

Bad waters icy afternoon
smooth jazz lapping walls
American desert surprises
hawk-eyed observer,
daughters of the imagination light lamps
in the spirit world,
tables fly
holy days sanctioned
red fox burrowed
on the western ridge
near redwood trees

loggers sanctified, breathless,
heartland memories drift,
dear friend, bad waters,
in an emergency parade
daughters step
out of the mind, O come now plumed
bird, plummet headlong crown
of thorns and shield of pale flowers,
radiant women,
bless mournful light,
on the wet path, heavy blades of grass
and mallard pond, headlights of silence
rule the highway

what are humans made of?
Beehive, blood, tranquil sleep,
green age, bum's rush, Blackbeard
barren hillside, immense
sawmills, "Becoming" no shadow
Blackbird, Blue, Bach

Brave luck, prayer wheel, piss
pill pot

blessed are the meek
who surrender shafts
of shadows on pale bough

sapling, famous twang
deluge erupts, false song,
common rocks scattered
over tombs, Beat drums

ANNEX TO "B"

musicians file-in,
the first violinist
will be better
tonight, she
elbows
across the orchestra,
trips over
a French horn

the oboe strays a
fraction, what manner
of animal
is man? where
is the beautiful
sentence?

authenticity is
what the conductor
practices, space
between tonal
altitudes, colors
of sound, tone is
the accelerator

music is thought
not feeling, tone
not simply a miraculous
tremor, music is color
not form, BUT
music is beyond, tones

in procession, tides
pulled by sun and
moon, better to
pay attention to
blue paeans
from a godless
pianist who
composes poetry
and philosophy
on the other side
of bitterness

trust harmony, visualize
each ton, organize
a bureau of sound

music, then, brings
men down to
confusing rhythms
out of fear and
severe idealism
resigned blood is
no longer sacred,
humanity bounces

up to now
a blade of light
sufficed, trim the
sound as it bellows

C

Catullus on a boat, Cat in the shade
pine trees do not vanish once night folds,
they do not go somewhere else,
birds enjoy their branches,
trunks continue to find roots,
they cool men of bad attitude
and cool the nerves

be calculating, may Sleepy Hollow
deliver the genius of death to our
poor limbs, in the air aromas sound
out, pine and ash, fungal clouds,
threatening roar of a waterfall
further up the path, step low into
the blood of language, do those
letters not float? are not the letters
individual arks?

to go underneath the average, to
pin down words that have risen
out of an inland sea, to listen as
the pine trees spin their ancient
codes, walk in circles, covert
reason into forested light, cool,
be sure how the miracles scale
over the esplanade, on a terrace
far away language looms, a breeze
kicks in, colors behave, cumulus
entices the condor, billows fall
in line, letters go to work

those pine trees remain despite
the hellish sawmill, cool, elegies
will storm men's minds, deep in
sorrow verse and nouns, pious
verbs must conquer pain, so good
so far, ideas are trees, metaphors
are splendid branches, cool the
sound, sing for silence, probe
cerebral night, nothing to love
or hate, who is "I" in the complex
machinery? what of words? when
does language come round at last?

ANNEX TO "C"

distances collapse
especially on Amtrak
speeding over bare
American bones
sleep comes easily
count sleep

cling to an "I"
count love
continue herding clouds
over chalk-brown peaks

D

deeds pile up
on the front porch
dauntless others
poke their heads in
drawn by rumor

decide to be good all hours
be good for keeps
terrible roads open up and

be sweet on the porch
guarding rows of petunias

decide oh a good dog
jump onto my lap
good day
profitable
so much goodness
a ma might faint
or pray for acrimony

nothing like boredom
damn
drops of doubt
nothing quite like smoke
to blow
up his ashes
nowhere to dig
but here
in hard dry soil

ANNEX TO D

timber birds split a sonnet down the pole
everyone takes notice
yet they busy themselves with barter
and deception, focus is lost, winter
arrives like a giant madman, now night
now day now busy doing nothing
now the timber bird speak
of the meaning of life, do demand
attention, grave concentration, divine
introspection, descend to the sidewalks,
ring a ride, be smug and crooked, show
no concern for the homeless shepherd

demons join the orchestra,
drummers go to work,
dead folk drift in Tule grass,
diamonds are a dozen in the market,
do you not see?
ring another ride,
order a glass of afternoon
before its too late,
press your lips to the gaping breeze,
dream on, prophet,
life is rain, the Delaware overflows

E

everything dumped
onto the field, every conceivable
trinket, the one who
notices turns away

everything soon forgotten,
a loud gray cloud hovers,
old goats struggle
to the tavern,
smoke soon rises,
emotions lay
hidden in leather

our daughters
run in joy over
the wharf, soon
the boats arrive
with onions,
lettuce and bell pepper

one afternoon
Lord Buddha will appear

and right every wrong,
for now a balance,
enough said, silence

or even the braying
of donkeys, enough!
language follows
men rise, the sun follows

F

those fakirs annoy less
now that men live forever

dream funnels of air
and wake up feeling older
than the stars

don't laugh!
think only positive ions
in the circulating biosphere
go hither
hitch a ride on an eagle
who hunts for prey

stay primitive
don't be sorry
let the good times be silver bells
made of tinfoil
as an ancient Indian trail reveals
the sacred flames

find peace on Saraswati's porch
where fire-roasted chestnuts await

cling to a generous flume
from Buddha who is the minister
of genuine appreciation

big fag for posterity
in humble waters

plain old flower beds
invite a caring hand

flow soft

touch an invisible spire
of pine
when the early frost
ramps

witness freedom—blast
free feeling—the orthodox apostles
knock—do not deny
their frailties—there is genius
when they talk
in the manner of reflected light

prove to the people
what is unseen—
jovial fields will reveal
good intentions

words hover—lovers
fall in sheets—stay blue
through these decades

chirping letters lead—fame
hides under a rock—fallow
the field follows form risen
bright speck—

yes, Buddha arrives
for coffee on the deck
where birds perform

ANNEX TO F

Fight for what is
you have that right
do not despair
you eyes are full of fruit trees
file a claim
be quick
do not worry about the movies
never fret

the yellow leaves of autumn
belong in a book
in the field of song

he lifted the blue bird
a blue-bird, bluebird, in
the dark of night
he fled, at dawn he
reached the French
border, in due time
it grew cold, the shining
science hit his lungs,
in a fever he lifted the cup
for the birds of prey

he made his way
through a city of shutters
and drains, a seaport,
men mended their nets,
snow on the high peaks
appeared to be burning
he chanted a Fire Sermon
to the assembled

assassins who blew smoke
up his chimney

you have the right to remain
in the Fire, stay Firm, be Fair, Follow love
wherever it goes, deepen your Fame
in the tidal pond, bright anemones
glowing, small purple bodies
dropping on glass

G

year by year a messenger-god
runs wild—last of a kind—lost glories—
midnight dies—hospital corridors
are empty—godless prophets awaken
unemployed—does anyone require
a miracle—guardians of the cave
come forward—grapple—turn
a phrase—the darkness invades
single letters

H

how beautiful to be at the beginning
of something

winter has arrived
it happens now and then
heavy noise
harmonious ripple
harmonium reverberating

here where art awakens
here where stars glitter
prophetic minds seize the hour

hello Helen of Troy
precisely bouncing
one idea against another
in airport lobbies, without

notice emptied hallways,
zones of indifference

hell here on earth
innocence drowns immense
ceremonies
        no one gets a pass, lights dim

hi!
how are you?

twisted knot of the Great Basin
surrounded by travel trailers
and cowboys with nowhere to go

hopeless, midnight restless,
sleepers awaken
in heavy waves of silence
help us
heed our warning
hydrogen winter a dread
mandolin of sound
where would we go?
hell is just around the corner

       you may not hide,
Satan and his sister arrive in town
       and rent a condominium,
I'm pouring wine

back up
the trouble begins in heaven, men suffer there
the suburbs keep on growing
schools and office complexes post office
nail salon perverts thieves evangelicals
icicles ice hype

here in hell granny has soap bubbles
in her private shrine and thick gray
carpets on her mind, no wonder
she has trouble moving
it's hailing, we run for cover, men say
how was I in the heat
easy to feel the fire

hell
people are born in tarpaper shacks
surrounded by luxurious malls,
their fathers become skeletons

nobody plays the trombone,
life is not long, here we are
jumping
through hoops, building our joints,
looking for heaven
but hell intervenes

men waste decades,
away on a piano
up in outer space
where it counts
such melodic pride
through a life
of courage and
sacrifice, so fine
is doom
this hydrogen
noon

harpist
be awake
hide nothing
be aware
help all men
hard are the chords
of the guitar
bruising ripe poetics
one more time

be led along
hell's laconic farm
where animals
see into the hearts of men
hell

hanging
hell
at the heart
hell
running

hell yes
no
flood famine roaring flames

"h" is a buzzard

ah! blizzard

heap of glass

fit the letters into a bag when tackling
the high pass, stop for a campfire, hot tea
and lentil soup, say hell to the light snow

ouch!

it's that damned star again, a star fashioned
in heaven and it comes (invades) every so often
hyper love low lean hyperactive hymn

I

real tragedy is hidden behind
drawn shades
Ruby remains
secrets wrapped in wallpaper
no one feels
nightly she sketches
autumn boughs—the yellow planks
fall from her thoughts

go easy—may she find
music from the radio—ads
astound joy—islands
abound—sometimes islands
are swept by cold wind—oftentimes
children run along shore chasing
seabirds—her memory of September
is idyllic—the archon sat on his throne
and mused over the islands
in his domain—authorities know
how to warn the coral reef
of the furthest island

rubies rheumatic
askew—turn on the fan—unfold
the morning's news—famous
movie star laid to rest—Korea sleeps
through rugged night—how long should
she live? a bracelet of palms on an island
far beyond—where goes innocence? how
does guilt figure? Ruby loves son and
daughter—she trains blackbirds

J

they smile in their lounge jackets
those jack-assess
under wise magnolia clouds
smooth music (the blues)
should have known better,
horn to horn, old color,
old colored light, odd covered
in spite of justice

they dine in spite of limber trees
as the snow gently slips-in a note or two

K

if not white, what then?
Hey, dig Krazy Kat,
if not red who would caboodle
down a hole
the rat's nest
and if not white or red
black might settle
a Jew in the nick of time
or a man from Bali
or Seoul or Oslo

dog kennel, get it?
at the root
a solid grounding

L

Look at that narrow window
in which the widow listens
to secrets of the city

she has no teeth

generations pass, she lives
for what others say, their slips
of tongue and secret passion

her neighbors speak over traffic—
not an impediment

she hears the old folks
in the Cadillac Hotel, a
likely group of assassins
and retired prison guards

look how beautiful they are
in that ill-upholstered lobby
she tells herself as she pets
Lollipop the Cat who has
perfect green eyes

look at the lonely doors
of their minds they wash
their dirty laundry night
and day

learn to gather sexual peccadillos

who is the lead predator?
leap across decades
of desire, Satan spells
bad advise, the shoemaker
is a middle-aged Jewish refugee
the Nazis yanked out his tongue
but still he sings

God is a window

Lilies thrive in the lily pond

Lucky Strikes

in her notebook
not a thing forgotten

God is a window

the widow never looses sight

SHE WILL NOT LET GO

life is a window

listen to "sometimes"
loop a lean rope lots of medication

the human cargo in the hotel stinks
of old age, they choke to death late night
Lights Out
lackluster final moments fly like gulls
onto the traffic

down on the boardwalk
the tram goes at 10 miles per hour

Liquid poetry

Poverty

Dread the hour

Luminous brain death

the universe is made of lavender
if you mind, or of bacteria and distilled
alcohol, whatever

turn on the Lamp

Light a sound

M

midnight middle of a color
moon-sign muddled words
music ah yes (!) MUSIC to sustain
every need

malic and the muse

moon-night-muddled sign—words—silence

mental fields of wheat
on the road south, out of Milano

oh Milano
when it is 94 degrees
a child walks out of the mirror
south
on the highway
to Bagnone

mind this musical note
hardly malicious, but tough

make no mistake in the science
of a mystical experience

up to the sepulcher a calm evening
little drummer boy and Tiny Tim
with Huckleberry Finn and Jack O Lantern

they are making haste

free-wheeling boys
eating noise and moving fast
so clouds don't catch them

it's how life is done, a light of
surreal machines
for mid-summer dreams
ODD THEMES COLD CLUES
LOST ILLUSIONS

mid-mind

ANNEX TO M

COLD WIND calls from a mountainside
where men worshipped
anointed harbingers of war
COLD WORDS touch stream's bank
I begin a pursuit of veracity
scattered like gems in a day-dream

COLD MOUNTAIN awakens early
to hear the morning doves converse
in cool and meditative strophes
COLD MOUNTAIN composes a twig
snapping again—never does this poet
consider putting down his lovely pen

COLD TERRACE where honor builds
despite perilous hours—pears are
heavy on their boughs—time trickle
COLD TERRACE for a Lord of Fire
grown wise in a traveling circus
that is all too real, and never ends

COLD PROPHET brings a golden lamp
for father and daughter—rage will
not rule—the bond only prospers
COLD PROPHET is a snowman
who thrives in the ice—summer
dines on promises of winter yet to come

N

the landscape trembled
when darkness obscured
bundles of new-mown
grass spread across the plain,
no further commentary
needed except the trip had
just begun, yet nobody
knew anything,
where were the people going?
never mind, mumble a catechism,
pretend to be the Pope or
Nazi General,
buy a parrot and
teach her how to pray in silence

only detonations
far back where cerebral fires roar
are required, the mind
commits war crimes
as the train picks up speed

Night travels Noon babbles
Nations rattle, No man
dare cross blindly
into the Forbidden Zone,
open a Pepsi-Cola
for eternity's sake,

outside the busted sewer,
deep depressions on the lawns, one
fig tree leaning on a stone barrier
trust is inedible, stacks of ambition

fill the garages, three junk cars out front
of a sad structure,
Nothing to show on the main highway

New road to a poetic fence
Nick of time
Nice to meet, now please don't speak

Leave time alone

Rooftop generation
of birds singing such songs
as tomorrow we've nothing to spare

Nature injects

National desire

Native moon

the nerves filter down

proud desert flower

prove these nascent powers

Naked now

"November Boughs"

knee-deep in travail, fevered train tracks,

philosopher, stand guard, letters are not easily
forgiven for insisting on existing independent

the conductor dressed in black, maintains a raven
who has red eyes that pierce the heart
and render men speechless

put the crystal in his palm
where it belongs

O

unroll the scroll and go to work on tiptoe, grab a noteworthy ditty
from stellar eyes, the benefits of life are incredible, a soul may go shopping
online or drive to the park overlooking an indifferent ocean, one may hear
trees talking shop, "*Ohm* your bark need a going over," "The sawmill is going
overtime," and so on until men are bent like nails, "open your heart," says
the Ash tree, "Go fuck yourself," roars Ponderosa Pine perched on land
above Lake Tahoe, O what men observe in a forest, O how land management
is a scientific endeavor, operate accordingly, pause at the creek, ominous
plants appear, lichen clings

unroll the papyrus, write until frost clings to window glass, wait on the horde
it will come to rush down the walls, offer incense to a quiet shaman who
meditates the long hours, he will hand over a twig, after the twig he offers
a leaf, when that is done the wealth of a rock randomly discovered, open doors
in the wet meadow, more conversations between the trees, for hundreds of
thousands of years they exchange information, O no! O yes! O my Lord! O come
put your higher branches into communion, the birds will flock to your side,
rainfall will summon your hidden aspirations

P

be wary of private property
and all it takes

*

paid for the island and
its birds, the sea tortoise,
paid for sand-grass, paid
for mind-junk, for degradation
of means, paid for night, "this
is my darkness, I have a bill
of sale," preliminary epic
of failure, PRIDE, proof of
dead feline, pricks in
beautiful automobiles

a pride of lions

please play fair
listen to cloud nine,
what fails to emerge
from behind us

*

Slim Pickens

*

heat from the pleasure-dome,
dirty old men

*

pack of liars dealing cards
on a half-hidden street
behind the old stables

*

field of abandoned cars
and snow-plows,
procure a godless road
and proceed, follow science
if you feel like it

*

dive for pearls
in this prosaic world
of sea-walls, plants die,
people thrive, pulsating lanterns
cover the eyes of a traveler

*

to the world of worms
to men of the book a breakdown
in communication:

wait for Z
Pray for X
go for Y
parade your lettered lives

there will be no delay, sir,
you may proceed
to your gate

*

tangled sidewalk light

*

the house is late
please forget us
prove a means, a methodology

*

I heard poems on the deck
coming from several points

*

admit the compass

*

PRINCE OF LIGHT
DO TURN OVER ALL
NECESSARY DOCUMENTATION

*

patience is called for
as you prepare for eternity
oh love linger loud and long

*

Papa! it snows tonight
the moon will freeze

*

I'll sacrifice pride
in deep snow on the rugged
baseline of reverie

Q

quintessential piling of stone
quiet mid-morning campfire
the rocks are hot
coffee boils

we rub our eyes
and smoke a bowl

R

inside of the red rose a bar
where drinkers come to be alone
they worship hard liquor and
cold beer and cigarettes and privacy
in the bartender's droopy eyes
seeds of failure and despair
though he keeps the bar clean
and pours an honest shot

so what became of William Blake
whose visions ripped men apart
whose words were born in
thunderous rapids? who traveled
with Red Riding Hood in the days of awe?
what lifeboat does one need
when crossing a "T" or harboring
a stealth of "R's" for breakfast?

the red rose howls, banners fly over
Samurai swords, the bartender's name might
come back, Ralph? Red? Rudy? o toothless
grin, oh cognac and beer, ah, rye whiskey,
table shuffleboard, sawdust in the heart
Babe Ruth hit the ball out of the park

re-arrange the sky if you have the cajones

ANNEX TO "R"

real colors collide, rapid red
slow-moving blue, green Umber duns
white window ocean
orange orchards, this spectrum

what more? sheep going down
a path well-worn, rugged cloud front
warns of trouble, an official hawk
skirts the headlands, coiled colors
veiled color, colors cut-out in hand-worn
gestures

real color, Matisse in a quiet moment
cuts a circle in the sky, really, one should
entreat the gods to paint a corner
as a thieving priest or violated alter boy
show the peeling stucco or like Rembrandt
two dots for eyes, black dots

colorless corner of the forest rich in dew and
green-gray bushes, rapid are the thoughts,
raucous the field mice, color the sun red,
so long to the old masters,
the are not of any value

some trembling old fool deep in debt
painted a detailed map of hell on earth,
a drooling idiot put a tag on pastoral terrain
framed in poplars
a flat-out pervert twisted women into shape,
what about Edgar Degas, forever counting coin?

be real! colors do nothing special,
they create a mean average,
yellow ties, dead blues, stay on track,
a grey or white cloud, silver bees, golden trees,
careless letters in a brown box,
violet, periwinkle, the glass at night,
rage on, read a book

S

the seasons weigh on her
as she hangs laundry, yard
filled with pomegranates, sweet
eyes, kind lips, terrifying planet
of waste and revolution, she
places a pair of pants, a towel

she wears green gloves,
her hair is long, pouring over
the shoulders, every article of
clothing is a banner or flag,
in some distant realm war
machines glitter

simple clouds pock the sky
above her, she is every mother
back then hanging the clothes,
keeping simple communion,
may the sun warm her cold
shoulders and allow each season
to build, may men one day
prepare for a difficult journey
down by an ocean of memory
and dream, down where
the true life begins

T

walk city streets on a Winter's day,
looking for the quiet cafeteria
where they held the Chinese lottery,
walk down a confusing grid of possibilities
until there it is, shabbier now, dusty
windows, weak lighting

in the old days men with black briefcases
fell in line, what a miserable line of work,
failed novelists used to sit at a corner table
comparing notes, trading tales of rejection

today is Wednesday, a day full of promise,
time philosophers had long promised,
self-publication could bring a wide readership
great fame, go down like Herman Melville
to the sinister ocean, spare no one,
we're only on the planet a short time
trim all excess,
tidy up the work space,
buy file folders,
clean the plate

think of it as a game that will not be lost,
compete with other commuter,
learn how to type blind-folded

below a Xmas Tree in Webster's Market
are loaves of bread, cartons of milk
and a pack of smokes
remember the cat, purring
the men of town

prize tambourines and tin drums,
they blast a hole in tenacity
and consider the imponderables
on their way to a heavenly home

pound the light, praise evil men who crash
and are drowned,
ask for rhapsodic noonday reveries,
wild visions, twisted versions of reality

U

up in the air

the wolf needs a home
so do certain powers
in the last decades
of human activity

*

make a U turn
in the nick of time

it is 35 miles
to the next meditation center
imagine falling despondent
and being unable to move

*

a quarter's worth of light
to spill over the panther's back

*

a human brain is wired
to the flower, the pretty
flower dances on
a grave, tie the knot, un-type
the last sentence

*

human error
wasted the bouquet
and shut down the banquet

*

slowly nature makes
its way sending white ash
and mass starvation
to the urban park

V

the leader lies under heavy slabs of marble
in broken land
vehement clouds rush to fill the empty halls
where language once made the hours pass
like movements in a symphony

violinist called to shatter the crystal
poised, her history is a lilac
her arms drift in remembrance of false dawn
no matter—pure music pours
like morning showers
on the heartland
victory! beautiful gardeners applaud

men know the beautiful nights
have vanished
Ernie's van dead on the lawn
he won the lottery but died
empty-handed
reaching for a hyacinth high
above body pain
hello mercy, bad dog!
who is the fairest martyr
of them all?

SHIN   ALEPH   GIMEL   LAMED

in every letter a flock of birds

yellow leaf come for grief

The book lay open, 'The Book of Psalms"
no path promising peace alone—war looms
on the tip of a pen—"The Lord is my shepherd"
over fields of poverty and spite—every letter shines
over those hills where wild goats survive

poetry is founded in a blue flame, an accident
barely noticed, apple trees are mute, baskets
of oranges await, the hewer of marble
wrote sonnets in praise of a defiant deity, oh jazz
rescue the miscreant, praise shelter from wrong-doing

the meaning of futility

BETH   AYIN   MEM   NUM

WHY   ZEE   ESS   LOOM?

a closed book

when was what matters most?

voluminous poem strung-out late at night

draw a death lance

weather-vein
bow and arrow
cross-bow
stone weapon
battle-ax
control of
the stratosphere

W

either or
winter is a wick
summer coming in
sing cuccu now wrap
willful speed
wick of what wham
whimsical whopper
true where trust withers
sing cuccu nu
in a tide of plague
of his bones
are coral made
handsome devil ceding night's
decrepit boy
out of deception spread
erotic
up above wisdom's gate
wise prayer men congregate
loud lute
abide umber wood side wake
why not?
water wrinkled dust
wreck racket wait on fight
wrangle free ecstatic whip
Western sea turtle
Midnight's spoiled brat
phonographic pornography
it came
world without a moral
code to handle guardians
sleeping
words voided by lack of trust

September's coronation long forgotten
tinsel torn, what moves
in lush noon? then the Evening Star
sparks a bitter debate in the woods

wait, wander, wait wander, dip a finger
in the well, wait on time, timid hours pass

welled up from a sacred grove
listen as the chorus provides
letters as assault weapons,
chill archaic
blame game fate presents
dilemma, draw
on chance, good men brought
down, wasted
thrown by the wayside

wait, WAIT, throw caution,
when memory
wandered aimlessly, when
oil lamps led the way
pluck petals from the wicked rose
ancient wisdom leaks

LOVE and some shallows,
dream sequence
widening the gap
stellar jays one more time—
they are beautiful
and annoying
wait for us!
our train is late,
we are still hoping

we maintain belief
despite all the chaos
win a word
off the slate
worshipper of stone
Wagon-Lit
(Philip) Whalen
whammy!
who would when wild?
dazzled warriors
woe-begotten
men are liars
to each other
what greater pain?
enter and be proud, set your mind
on this swirling whirl,
wish for handsome bough
rigid, unyielding, reach
leaves
lonely wolver-what? wattles

WHAM!
woman men
oh

WRITE IT DOWN

TRIM EXCESS

X

xylophone is priceless
like the diamond
at The Palace of the Legion of Honor
encased in a walnut box
across from Renaissance paintings

when the musician played
harps became restless
men in uniform passed in review

what is not beautiful?

what remains of old empire
and sacred dimension?
why ask?

your eyes are tools for solitude,
the tones conform
to colors spread over rough
and dangerous terrain

Y

yes and no he muttered
to his landlord, I've looked
everywhere and cannot find a thing

not underneath the morning newspaper
drawers are empty, hope dangles

chattering primates invade
the living room

hail beats on the tin roof
of a storage shed across the alley

here is a brick wall,
the yew tree trail, young forever
under the shadow of a grieving deity

travel light
from front room to the toilet
or when exploring a closet
where God protects moths

generous earth is of no help
seasons re-arrange the shadow

laughing Buddha is a front porch
yelling at kids to slow down

curse and yell, it won't matter,
certain laws are unwritten

friends come and are shocked
at the lack of care

or of sincerity, no wonder
the rugs look so dreadful,
please go away, may these coming years
be fruitful,
may the yearling pass in peace

Z

possible, yes, but when
those myrtles combine
Zion gathers ethereal sleep
from zoo to zoo from shield
to shadow, Zen koans
make waves, cry or laugh
draw shadows from fields
beyond those walls

"now we speak of miracles"

"at the zenith, simple miracles
    sewn by common angels"

of a kind,
zealots, they perch on every balcony
whispering vanities—men are selfish
twisted noon beacons ZAP
again, zigzag
a path to the monastery

past the ziggurat's

shallow pond—

careless storm—tranquil streams
become raging river, danger everywhere

at the zenith
cool meridian

a sundial

in the courtyard

peacocks strutting
blue
     and green, red and yellow

for any trees a mist
    decorum
       grace, a plan for changes
in weather
   and disposition

   zoom! ZOOM, deft hand
over gardens of desert

poise
    ZING
   allow passage
     into the mind

   zip up the sky
    terns
   following
    the rumor
      of an authoritative demise

ABC's 2

IN MEMORY JACK HIRSCHMAN

AB

four white petals
red fold of petals
one yellow, gathered

wilted gardeners

fine woven flowers
in a bouquet offset

by spiked red smoke,
trembling arms of
the florid man who

pours water, listens
as hungry plants
fight for existence

on glass table-
top, look how cats
curl nearby surprised

by essence, beguiled
color, look at loud
reflections, closely

guarded martyred
petals press
process at least

one billion years
in the making,
men seem bothered

having to wait,
why do they dive and
snap? lithe precious tone

of color, dappled faint
chlorophyll seething
out of the bouquet

to earth's edge,
row after row
of imperial ivory,

cypress, stone caught
in grief, send
daisy by express love

for black birds
who skip over fences, see

marshland deer, speckled
clouds, mangrove pulling
brackish sea

so goes the

I am realistic concerning death
but less so on the telephone

anguish clings
to white wounds
on butterfly wings

find the sun
on my wrist

super-flare

come upon
bent coin
by plants,
salute grapevines
giving zinfandel
to the human zoo

count zero as a charm

tumult spills
out of sound

will Joseph endure
in spite? trace
the Nile to its source

oh children in a hurry
woman cradling
her child near quick
granite clouds
red on hillsides

turn left at two bridges
be quick

seek out a passage
on primal ground, pine needles
and chipmunks abound

squirrels wear fancy duds
as they climb

pass barbed wire
of a military base
Sinai of an abandoned
hotel, railroad town
Barstow

poor mother nature died
of processed food
on ramparts, must everyone
blame her
for the enemies
racked up over time?

yes go sleep
on nettles, go commune

echoes of travelers
foreign skies, diet
on highway to Vegas
don't mind, 110
degrees climbing wall
of pale stone, did you ever
read "The Desert Music?"

cat scratches fiddle

hum goblin will getcha

descend from summit
devotion glows
against silent
sun-drenched roses

waitress in a donut
sugar honey pie

tonight

words drip

taste feeling

eat the cloud tonight

language gives up
as folk chat it up

what part of death
joins you for coffee
pre-dawn?

pass the World War Two
flag of pleasure, sign-up
for truth serum

love is an ice cube

island light

slow
dazzling explosive
idyll

drop voices at the gate

branches on the sun burn
slowly day by day

flock of songs in his fist

Z is for helicopter

Zebra is for snooze

past memory driven

"the sustaining air"

funeral of the world, unreadable
historical fiction

little slip of verse

spoken word time
when zebras die on the plain

Cd

see the place
where men lie and
get away with it

these trees
conspire as
demons live here

birds who dive
on this planet filled
with labyrinths
and dead ends
lies well-honed
talon-like

find autumn and
the so-called glories
of the season, I think
you enjoy twisting
creation, we see you are
made for untruth
you can seal everything in
your possession, I
will walk down to the ocean
thinking November
and those who seemed
out of their minds as gulls
cruise the shore and
you could not fault
them, you were
so concerned and so selfish
all you could do is talk

about yourself and
not listen to others

yes we outnumbered
birds,
difficult to understand
nearly impossible
to control how
not enjoyable to navigate
confusing ideas strange
rituals and then
stretch out on the grass
because silent November
amuses

the sky slowly murders
everyone of us,
clouds are not
smiling rage
will cause flooding

people will die

Ef

look and see come
round again don't
knock just enter as if
you own the place

ashes of a sonnet
shattering grace
line territory
of the fox, liquid moon
over our beds,
we are berries
and snake
were never
satiated, madmen

threw rocks at
us, we learned how
to fight back, racism
ruled,
meadows said
not a word, green
on green
in excess, bone
white black root, orange

handsome god
of fire, loud daughter
where water rages,
silent son, alas
crow-man, crowded
slave, born to
travel limitless space,
part the galaxies

as you stare, how
do we sleep at night
red hot fever in
plain sight?

when you stop and think
about it you actually "do"

these rivers and trees
brought us to a race at
the mouth of the river

this incredible sunset
ozone rip a tear in
sobriety

light belongs to
you because you fight
for it and recognize
that you are unrelenting

why did you kill the poet?
give us one good reason
for doing such a thing and
on Sunday of all days
day of our short fog
and triple sunlight and the moon
that won't go away on a
day when elk nibble
at seaside grass

why did you bother
to stab the poet multiple
times and to declare

your hatred of poetry?
what made you so
motivated? I would hope that
in the future men will take a
deep breath

hold on to propriety
and walk at cliffside

face a clear sea breeze

gulls ripen rude shore
east into sobriety
down slope
fern canyon
sea soul sound soft
salt
stanzas
build meditative breath

trio twinkle true blood
seeping cross a heart
in heroic hours
when the gods struggle
to bring the harvest in

go to sleep

EF ANNEX

the color yellow

every chance a
free passage
green hillside
saw gray shade
of goat we mean

whatever turns,
a passageway
down to waterways,
so long true color

that sky over Buenos Aires
seen from the window
brave colors
kaleidoscopic, look out
of dream

I imagine we're trying hard
to imagine anything, that's
hallway of seats and passengers
cation

millions of after thought
the smoke in unseen places
a walk on brown platforms
orange glow of a sudden
massive sense disconnection
we travel light we sound out
every fantastic wave

dark charcoal print deep
limestone glint rough morning
paper crane in pink lines
born to the emptiness a jar
of red pain jarring notes
mindful reflection loose change
offer no space lightening speed
the face of vermilion walk
in the park spill the ink
over her chest of drawers

a chance look fire lens
color book on coffee table
green world splendor turquoise
webbed onto forest

how light pale passion blue
flame
tumble down eyes
offer prayer
for early light

Gh

Kenneth we know
must change and we have
learned the limitations
of our fellow men and when
we look into the mirror
all we can do is jump in and
blaze a trail through the
brush land it is so difficult
to know which way to
go how to move with any
sense of grace or devotion

look for the mountains
find anger and
acceptance beautiful
to walk Flower-Wreath Hill
beside you when you are an
elder and to brush
days aside I did paint
the sky any
color I wish so free, feel
this morning walking
through your words
thinking what would he say?
how would he open
the day and what would
he do to bring it to a
grand conclusion? I
guess he would kick
the pinecone as I do passing
the bison paddock

Golden Gate Park yes
would not put it past him oh
man thou shall not kill but
it is what some
people do that kind
of sport as the
wind whips again
against coastal trees

see each individual tree
as crucial to the rhythm

inlets, black rock
embankment, mute
breakers, colony of
sea lions

why must land
turn orange? blast hole
on time, Dali's clock melts
in my arms

IJ

I went to read trees
to see you then
as you might guess
to see humpback whales
on the horizon
we waited on a high
bluff, hang gliders
passed before
charming clouds

later came gulls
dressed in
ceremonial robes
beating on drums
until the entire coast
began to chant

whine down

off the odd block

is that the ocean?

read for light here
in the ruins of
a volcano

body of robin red-breast

meadowlark blue surface

everything unseeable

scrape crystals
from window shield
child on the dream

KL

Baudelaire's mother peeks
into the garden

no never
not a pack of lies
entangled in the fishing
nets, only the ghost
of an angry poet
pacing medieval halls

Arcane

bless this father
who carries lantern
before dawn shakes
like pumpkin

I thought words served strong
sea-breezes over
green ribbon of desire

trade gray headlands as
humpback whales
climb into the sky before
plunging back

absorbs every curve

bird in another country

raven racing
pastel crags
Bryce Canyon

snow in the sunshine and rain
abundance starvation
one ridge

keep us informed

move pawn with decision

city stone by stone

sunlight stoplight

Gertrude Stein

demand an accounting
from the dreamers

life is music from a distance

today mercy

never fear angelic choir

plug your ears

Mn

designer phone
xylophone sundown
draw morning light
on the burning sand

flowers on the moon
do you see them growing
tall and handsome

single tree on earth
trust moon flower at all costs
if you think DNA is a matter of time
look at the stars
when the breeze comes
butterflies hum

how old are these apes
caged in the dark?

speed bump
gasoline everywhere
oh beloved
keep wide awake
your eyes on
the road ahead
until you are tried convicted
and sent to the penitentiary

wake up wake up
so you may fly above grief

sleep! toss and turn
as these shrouded hills
welcome oncoming spring

sleep!
offer no excuses
as we become tied-up
in huge rock formations
on the lonesome road
going home
to Grand Junction

sleep!
beloved poet so do you
grow old so piety sweeps
into your eyes
be again a light
on your mother's brow

Mn Annex

what is the call?
yellow fire
blue's vast courtesy
a sky of burning bushes
burning sienna umber lips
tremble deft arc light shaft blown
too
long
dope
drop
demand to read
fine dappled forest green
black as
ice

flow, windows
window trade bright
brass eyes serpentine
compassion torn
most silence
pain brush of gold
oranges in a basket
wicker fingers negro mind
reddish yellow

five doors blue doors

shut canvas
lulled true morning music

wave me more wind

window steppingstones

my passion was
for seemingly endless
stretches, bare
bones clouded sky

red white and
blue are the stresses

fingerprint green
and primary light

brace for
a series of haiku
like color
the o in
your dream
the a on the
tip of your tongue

brace for
conformity
the comfort zone,
what we know
flies over lava

brace for
rain fires forest breeze
coffee colored
atmosphere
on time's brocade

brace for
the computer routine
a comic poke the
laws that matter
when smoke clears

brace for
the changing world
on coastal road shadow sun
sun shadow a new moon

brace for
ridge route ceramic farm
the kids playing with desire
down a deep chasm of hope

Op

x is formidable
you go for x-rays
down a hallway
in an aged hotel
where men live like animals
and urine rules
alongside rats

I'll find Garcia Lorca
strumming a moon
in one of the rooms
handsome young sailor
in his arms

zip zap
what do you think of miracles?
why do you imagine
they are yours for the asking?

turn off those lima
bean fields before
late afternoon blots
all memory

QR

all I have is Abraham
the mythic bookbinder

your son is named Joseph
Bookbinder, we live in
crowded building on
a street in the Bronx
precious little help
for us even when we
pray for neutral ground

St

if the rain is heavy
and there is a catastrophe
try to sit in your studio
and write a poem
about the river, yes
impose yourself
on the mirror, try to understand
what it means to understand

one of those from Purgatory
to a wasteland oh
remain positive at any cost

Uv

these letters were crafted
by heavenly girls

get up at 5 am
and walk the rain
to a convenience store
for coffee and
a tuna sandwich

you want poetry
or prophecy?

do not hand us
gibberish

make a b-line
to ruthless imitation

if the butterfly has white wings
what do you propose?

I salute you who holds
viable truth before splendid
window glass, open a window
to clear your misery

sing again?
able to hear
the thunder
over rough ridge?

love jasmine
and morning coffee

build morning fire
because it is cold
and rub our hands
then we watch
as the sun moves quietly
across the redwood trees
and down the canyon
and under the massive bridge
and out to sea

Wx

Shelley
bitch, your poems
sweeten the flowing
river of words
to excess, go ahead
and cry but you should know
Tony Angel died

beg you write sweet paean
of hate, bare your anger
at the men who struggle
on Sourdough Ridge
go ahead and grab
a cab to the
last gathering

Crazy Jack was sweet
died in the bughouse

he was the mask maker
of Sunset Boulevard
before dragging himself
to New York City
a ragged Cheshire cat
16th Street
blessed Fernando
autumn's brow
cheek to cheek
Submarine Sam
beauty salons

Ralph with
new teeth

lanky moose, odd
lotus of the wilted
wink bam! all types
poetry lessons
poverty, oh Miss
Market Street
loony tunes lost
bleeding

roses
dainty-faced
genies

Coco Vega
at the prom
cruising
funny boys

you wrestle
boulevard
Miss Diana
Ross beautiful
art we are

fly off
we should
leave a bench
in the park, though
you would darn socks

I cross the street
enjoy that
Upper Castro view
in the morning
jazz

lower rungs
of Zen, animal
garden in the cold
moon step
with care

yon glare
glass of broken
ribbon
rooftop damn gate
shut no way
no way out of
devotional on to
own insidious
angel perched
at the edge

grab a rope
and pull
Miss Shelley
lady man
in an iron lung
my boyfriend
endured the
pain; we were
in the midst
of a plague

or a boy
he stayed three nights
in Lord Byron's cottage
where I kept
immodest diary
for future reference

oh Percy oh mercy
I'll scratch poems
and scramble images
from the dream

Tony Angel died
after forty years
of abuse, he was
the third son of
a Greek oil
merchant

splendid sad comrades
please don't die
tomorrow, avenge
the super subway
come listen
the trains clang

I'll break stone
on the expressway
and hitch a cab
from JFK

the sun was 25
years old, John Keats
is gone

oh Percy
you perfect
bitch oh
imperfection
hold on
wide eyes
of shires and
lay down our lives
on firm and pallid
ground near to
the Bay of Poets

tomorrow the architect arrives
he will consider when to
begin the ultimate meditation
how about atoms ancient pleasure
yes why not admit
the soft breeze through
heavy oak, why not build
Granada in one day?

pay attention to the joints
let men be free to die
in narrow beds
as the cathedral rises

sleep!

a glass of rhyme
will do, consider also
a bolt from the blue

think only of
glass, think of mirrors
and windows, build
a cemetery on the back acreage,
be sure
never to die

may other men perish

bury silence and sadness
on your plot
of land, hold firm
to the shovel,
say goodbye
to electrician
and rock musician

woke up praying
to prevailing angels
tangled up in blue mist

Men love old age
it should not
be missed

Yz

nothing much here
but alfalfa
in orderly stacks
from Parma
to your beating heart

w is what?
double your poem
with historical doubt
and future rage

w for quiet night
here in
the higher
light, thanks
for incomprehensibility
on these twisting
mountain roads

trust the window
frame and stained
glass, bring
the marbles
home

what the thunder refused to say
as the crabbers set forth,
this old man
the moon man responded
impolitely, a shadow
and stench fell over
the land, peasants

ate potatoes in candlelight
while the orchestra played
Beethoven's Ninth

join revelation of jasmine
make no deal
with desert deity
in the city of suspicion

toss ashes
on deserted beach
near Sea Ranch
o children of desire
the sky
gently rumble Whitman
pounds it out
gray smoke covers
his solitude

Gerard that'll be enough wood
for one night's fire, enough
shadow to fill these charms
and boundary lines
yes we ought to know
one more spinning wheel
out on the deck, plenty
of shade, yes enough
colors, we should know
enough by now, night comes
to conquer, let us have
enough history, this melancholy
you write on pours down
we hear Manhattan sober
in the background, one man

elegiacally imprisoned, he
gathers echoes, why not
walk courageously over
to the parkway, tell me
if this is the right stop, we
take the Grand Army elevator
to the last possible stretch
of land, here you are, this
is not the Bronx, we've been
looking for Queens, you see
we have a small plot, here
is Brooklyn, up in the attic
they've brought the nude
body of a famous artist who
died young

his passing made millions,
oh Gerard bend over
backwards
the truth I feel, infectious
fears blocking sight
as we awaken,
meant to see what
means facing memory.
listen to a
dream down by my boots.
history is not something
to trust. we become
disoriented walking
streets asking for
directions, nobody seems
to understand. why don't you
go two blocks straight ahead.
there is no Grand Army.

"

Brooklyn looms.
graciousness survives
in the details. remember
to close the gate every time
you leave, do not forget
forgiveness.
when you are downcast
it's best to move.
don't stay alone in the cell.
may I push you into a new reality?
come, Gerard, how we are old,
yesterday garage fell on my right leg
and now I am hobbling.
should go see the doctor
but mad, now we have
this new virus leaking
over life

congratulations.
thank you for this
treatise on melancholia.
thank you for the cottage
of Edgar Allan Poe
in the Bronx.
let me offer my thanks
for this volume of poetry
that can only be a
treasure like any
other box of opals.
life may only be a prism
if you allow it to be. what
if it was a
walk in the woods? let me

show you where I built a
'temple of grass.
a nest, are you holding a
cat in your arms?
go home, poet, go home to
shadows of light, trek these last
yards, walk cobblestone
take a photo of the Brooklyn Bridge,
words are melancholy
right from the start, the tots
play Ring the Rosie,
write more
elegiac fire for the fire cat, go
home to what you have
built with your own hands.
that'd be enough
for one life to manage

on the smooth grass
a gazelle

heaven blood

sleep trooper!
sleep on
a bed of chrysanthemums
on the island of Crusoe

what?
oh the ABCs

handle those ribbons

Ulrich Rabe

NEELI CHERKOVSKI grew up in Los Angeles where he edited *The Anthology of Los Angeles Poets* with Charles Bukowski and Paul Vangelisti. He moved to San Francisco in 1974 where he was associated with Jack Hirschman, David Meltzer, Lawrence Ferlinghetti, Gregory Corso, and a whole tribe of poets. His essay collection *Whitman's Wild Children*, originally published in 1989, with expanded subsequent reissues, provides intimate portraits of many of these contemporaries. In 2019 he co-edited *The Collected Poems of Bob Kaufman*, another close friend. Cherkovski's poems have been translated into Italian, German, Spanish, Turkish, and French. His most recent poetry collections are *Elegy for my Beat Generation* and *Hang onto the Yangtze River* (Lithic Press, Fruita Colorado). His *Round Your Tongue: New and Selected Poems, 1959-2021*, is also forthcoming from Lithic Press.

Made in the USA
Coppell, TX
07 November 2024

39811805R00069